Swim

By Jacinta Hayden

Library For All Ltd.

Swim

First published 2023

Published by Library For All Ltd
Email: info@libraryforall.org
URL: libraryforall.org

Our Yarning logo design by Jason Lee, Bidjipidji Art

Original illustrations by Fariza Dzatalin Nurtsani

Swim
Hayden, Jacinta
ISBN: 978-1-923110-18-2
SKU03342

Swim

We respect and honour Aboriginal and Torres Strait Islander Elders past, present and future. We acknowledge the stories, traditions and living cultures of Aboriginal and Torres Strait Islander peoples on this land and commit to building a brighter future together.

How do you swim?

Backstroke

Breaststroke

Butterfly

Dog paddle

Kickboard

Freestyle

Sidestroke

Underwater

Float

You can use these questions to talk about this book with your family, friends and teachers.

What did you learn from this book?

Describe this book in one word. Funny? Scary? Colourful? Interesting?

How did this book make you feel when you finished reading it?

What was your favourite part of this book?

About the author

Jacinta is from the Whadjuk/Noongar Nation and grew up in Merredin. She lives in Perth, and loves to yarn and share stories. When she was young, she loved *Green Eggs and Ham*.

Darwin

NORTHERN
TERRITORY

QUEENSLAND

WESTERN
AUSTRALIA

SOUTH
AUSTRALIA

Brisbane

NEW SOUTH
WALES

Perth

OUR YARNING

Adelaide

Sydney

ACT
Canberra

Author's Country

VICTORIA

Melbourne

TASMANIA
Hobart

Our Yarning

Want to discover more books from this collection? Our Yarning is a collection of books written by Aboriginal and Torres Strait Islander peoples across Australia.

We know that children learn better, and enjoy reading more, when they see themselves in the stories, characters and illustrations of the books they read.

To download the app, visit the Google Play Store on any Android device and search 'Our Yarning'.

librforall.org

www.ingramcontent.com/pod-product-compliance
Lightning Source LLC
Chambersburg PA
CBHW042345040426
42448CB00019B/3407